NEVER FART IN FRONT OF A CAT!

Poems and rhymes exploring
the relationship between
humans, animals and the world.

by T. Owen

Published by New Generation Publishing in 2024

Copyright © T. Owen 2024

First Edition

The author asserts the moral right under the Copyright, Designs and Patents Act 1988 to be identified as the author of this work.

All Rights reserved. No part of this publication may be reproduced, stored in a retrieval system or transmitted, in any form or by any means without the prior consent of the author, nor be otherwise circulated in any form of binding or cover other than that which it is published and without a similar condition being imposed on the subsequent purchaser.

Paperback ISBN: 978-1-83563-222-2
eBook ISBN: 978-1-83563-223-9

www.newgeneration-publishing.com

New Generation Publishing

Foreword

This collection of poems has been inspired by my love of animals, of nature and of the world in which we all live and how we interact with it and each other. I have tried to do this in a humorous but also thought-provoking way to hopefully raise awareness of the frailty of life and the fragile balance that exists between mankind and the world.

By exploring our similarities with animals and our dependency and interconnectedness with them, my hope is that there will be a greater harmonious relationship with our fellow earth dwellers and a renewed compassion for all.

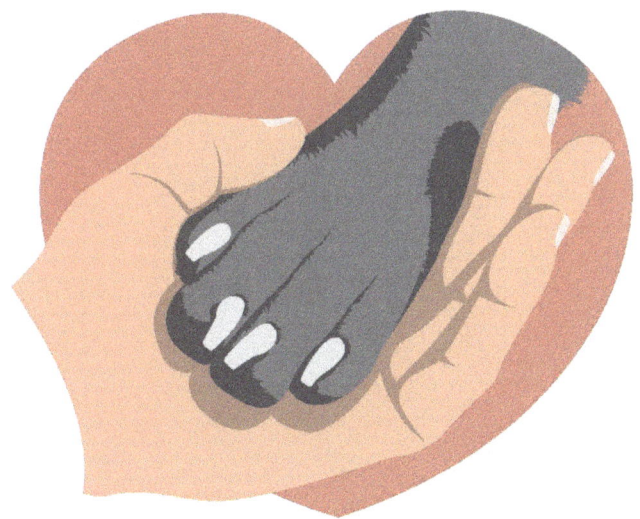

Never Fart In Front Of A Cat

Never fart in front of a cat,
Or let one rip or drop a bat.
They'll stare at you in great disgust
Because you bent and did a guff.
Then fix you with a baleful glare,
"How very dare you foul my air!"
They'll leave the room with haughty sniff,
Horrified by your naughty whiff.
Off they'll go into the night
To tell their friends of their dire plight.
"You know her at number twenty?
She rips rump and trumps aplenty."
And if perchance they should return
To stare once more with utter scorn
And fill the room with 'Eau de Mouse,'
Remember that it's not your house!
You are of course their merest slave,
Housekeeper, servant, lowest knave
On which to blame *their* fishy wind.
"It can't be me for I'm a king!
I once graced Egypt on the Nile
And had a comfort-filled lifestyle.
It was you that blew the tuba,
Now fetch my bowl of finest tuna!"
So, if a feline rules your home,
These words please heed, I do bemoan,
To keep your dignity intact,
Never Fart in front of a cat!

24th Oct 2016

Thank You For The Mouse's Head

Thank you for the mouse's head,
Bloody, grim and very dead!
The beady eyes still wildly stare,
The little teeth exposed and bared.

Thank you for the sparrow's feet,
No more to hop with cheerful cheep.
The tiny claws so small and hairless,
I'm really sad that you don't care less.
*"All things bright and beautiful,
All creatures great and small."*

Thank you for the wet intestines,
Lying there for me to step in.
Grey and wobbly on the mat,
Thank you, dearest darling cat!

Thank you for the tiny wings,
This poor dead bird no longer sings.
Shining feathers that once beat-
Lying there beside the feet.
*"All things wise and wonderful,
The lord God made them all."*

Thank you for the smallest shrew,
Its pointy nose covered in goo.
Its velvet coat all coarse and dry,
I am so sorry you had to die.
Thank you for the horse's head,
Bloody, grim and in my…. BARRY!!

20th October 2016

Barry (aka Barry White) was a neighbour's cat who left home and tried his hand at going feral for a while. After a few months of living in derelict shipyard barns and dining out on scraps found in refuse sacks, he decided to call on me to see if I would like to share my home with him! How could I refuse!?

He lived with me for a few years and was always his own man. A totally free spirit, he came and went as he pleased. He would often join me and my Greyhound Storm and Westie Glen on walks, coming so far with us then stopping off by the old dry dock, only to rejoin us again on our return home. Sometimes he would hide behind the Whitebeam tree on the green and leap out on us as we passed by. We always knew he was there and what he was planning to do but it was a prank that never grew dull for him.

A friend once stayed overnight to look after the dogs for me, and Barry decided to curl up with her all night. A few days later, she came for a visit, whereupon Barry pointedly ignored her and her advances. Turning his back to her, he left the room without a backwards glance. My friend was deeply hurt and felt as though she had been unceremoniously jilted. Barry obviously thought that their nocturnal tryst had been nothing more than a one night's stand!

Sadly, he has now passed on but he will remain firmly in my heart forever. He was my muse for a while and for that, I am eternally grateful.

Antibodies

Anti-bodies is such a misnomer,
Without them you might be in a coma (or worse!)
Patrolling your system like cops on the beat,
Looking out for harm from your head to your feet.
Disease and viruses, pathogenic bacteria,
Antigens all afeared in a state of hysteria
As a protein shaped like a flux capacitor
Latches on for the kill- it's the task it's for!
So, when next you marvel at the state of good health you're in,
Give thanks and high praise to this immunoglobulin!

18th October 2023

At least 60% of all known causes of disease are shared between humans and animals and around 75% of all emerging infectious diseases can be transmitted between humans and animals.

The Enemy Within

I don't care if you have two legs or four,
I'll invite myself in through the back door,
In your bones your blood and organs I'll dwell
And when the time's right I'll give you sweet hell.

I don't care if you're young or if you are old,
When I get a grip I'll not loosen my hold,
I'll silently wait; a thief in the night
And if given the chance, strike you from sight.

I don't care if you're weak or if you are strong,
Mutation's my game and I'll do you wrong.
My numbers now stand at one in just two,
So, watch out my friend, I'm coming for you.

18th November 2023

Cancer doesn't care what species you are. There are hundreds of different types of cancer indiscriminately affecting humans and animals around the world. Some are so similar, that a professional pathologist would really struggle to tell if the sample came from a human or an animal.

The Peace Within

Listen quietly, go within,
Close your eyes and just tune in.
The answers lie deep in your knowing,
Your third eye sees so watch it growing.

One breath in and one breath out.
Peace is what it's all about.
Do not force it- simply let it be
And in good time you will truly see.

Relax your body, find the calm,
Wrap in a blanket to keep you warm.
One breath in and still the clatter,
One breath out to lose the chatter.

Thoughts will come, just let them go,
Slow, deep breaths, flow with the flow.
Unwind the tension through every limb
And you will find the noise will dim.

Ground your feet, come back to now,
This is where you make a vow,
When life gets tough you find this feeling
And you've a path to peace and healing.

For Jillip.
18th December 2023

The Oak Tree

Many Winters you have stood,
Bravely facing wind and flood.
Your sturdy back braced against time,
Shrugging off the cold and rime.
Sleeping soundly, holding ground,
Whilst storm strewn saplings lie around.
Mighty oak tree there you stand,
Majestic symbol of this land.

Many Springs on you, have sat,
The power flowing in your sap.
Strength and courage in your veins,
Reaching outwards- all to gain.
Every fibre tuned and honed
Pulsates with nature's vibrant tones.
Mighty oak tree there you stand,
Majestic symbol of this land.

Many Summers you have seen
Nesting birds in leaves of green
Fill your world with busy days,
As you bask under glowing rays.
Early dawns and balmy nights
Transcending you to lofty heights.
Mighty oak tree there you stand,
Majestic symbol of this land.

Many Autumns have passed by,
With frosty air and moonstone sky.
Paling sun warms golden locks
As you attest the seasons' clock.
Holding on to those so dear,
Shelter secured for the next year.
Mighty oak tree there you stand,
Majestic symbol of this land.

Many years for you assured,
The cycles turn for many more.
The seasons merging into one,
Lessons learned and wisdom won.
Standing square your journey proved,
Acorns attest life's path pursued.
Mighty oak tree there you stand,
Majestic symbol of this land.

09th February 2007

A Caged Hen

Caged Hen
Omelettes, scrambled and poached
CLUCK!!

20th October 2023

The oldest chicken ever recorded was 22 years old when she died, although the normal life expectancy of a well-kept chicken is around 15 years of age. Hens can lay eggs for up to 5 to 10 years.

However, commercial laying hens are only allowed to live for around 20 months. Broiler chickens are killed when they reach their target weight which is at about 40 days old. There is no commercial value placed on male chicks, so they are killed when they are only 1 day old.

Howlin' Dog Blues- A Shaggy Dog Story

Woke up this morning to a terrible sound,
Looked out of my window on Hell's slathering hound.
He pursed up his lips and his howl rent the air,
My legs went to stone and white turned my hair.
Oh Lord, won't you please hear my desperate cry?
I've got the howlin' dog blues and I don't want to die!

If you spell dog backwards you come up with God
But there aint nothin' holy 'bout that hairy great sod!
He bristles and snarls and he's covered in mange,
My head it is spinning and I'm feeling quite strange.
Oh Lord, won't you please hear my desperate cry?
I've got the howlin' dog blues and I don't want to die!

He's pacing about and he's doing his nut,
Oh please keep me Lord from Satan's pet mutt!
He's baying for blood and he's pawing the ground,
I can't stand much more of this spine- chilling sound.
Oh Lord, won't you please hear my desperate cry?
I've got the howlin' dog blues and I don't want to die!

He's been at it all day and well into the night,
His curdling whines give me such a fright.
Now the moon it is rising and things will get worse,
I'm under the spell of his terrible curse.
Oh Lord, won't you please hear my desperate cry?
I've got the howlin' dog blues and I don't want to die!

Now they say a dog's bark it is worse than his bite,
But I've seen his teeth so I'll keep out of sight.
His fangs they are shining and he's grinning with glee,
He's looking for dinner; I just hope it's not me!
Oh Lord, won't you please hear my desperate cry?
I've got the howlin' dog blues and I don't want to die!

He's mooching about and he's raided the bin,
Oh please keep me Lord from this canine of sin!
He's lying in wait and he's stalking the cat,
He leapt in the air and he just caught a bat.
Oh Lord, won't you please hear my desperate cry?
I've got the howlin' dog blues and I don't want to die!

Now stakes are for vampires- maybe werewolves from hell?
A fillet, a sirloin or a T bone done well,
I've raided the fridge and I've thrown him some meat,
Now he's fast asleep and curled at my feet!
Oh Lord, thanks for hearing my desperate cry,
I've had the howlin' dog blues but I'm not going to die!
The howlin' dog blues but I'm not going to die!
The howwwwlin' dog blues but I'm not going to die...!

16th August 2006

The Seasons of Life

Snowy heads peep from the earth,
Nod shyly to the dawn.
With promise of a happy birth
They welcome in the morn.

Speckled breast in emerald green,
A song to lift the soul.
Often heard but seldom seen,
We look in bough and bole.

Listen how the bees do drone,
Their pockets full of gold!
Weave a dance, then fly off home,
A story to be told.

Sit awhile upon the ground,
Lie back and feel the warmth.
Summer's crushed green velvet gown,
Her skirts swirl o'er the Earth.

Close your eyes and fill your head
With weaving, dancing light.
Tumbling leaves of bronze and red
Proclaim a southward flight.

Time to reap? Still time to sow!
The cycle never ends.
Pass along all that you know
To family and friends.

On the world a blanket lies,
Muffled, cold and deep.
Curled within we will not die,
Protected- all asleep.

Unfurled once more our faces turn
Towards the bright new day.
The light shall shine for ever more,
In God/ess we trust and pray.

For Yvonne.
17th March 2005

'The Seasons of Life' was written in dedication to my mother Yvonne Slater upon her death and was recited at her funeral. After the service, I was approached by Megan Colledge- a cousin to my mother. She commented upon the fact that my grandfather had also written poetry. I replied that I knew he had but had never read any of it, having been told by my mother that it had been burned after his death in 1962. Megan then solved a forty-three-year-old mystery by proclaiming that she had my grandfather's notebook! It had been presented to her mother Naomi Burgoyne (my grandfather's only sister) by his wife Dorothy, following his death, as a memento of her brother. Megan has very kindly passed this collection of twenty-three wonderful poems to me.

The following three poems were penned by my grandfather and deserve a place in this collection. The third, not least, for it is believed to have been written for my mother when she was still a young child.

Reminiscences

I oft sit and dream of my young childhood days
Midst nature so splendid in various ways,
When with my companions in one happy band
We wandered the mountains, so lofty and grand.

As there on the summit we all stood and scanned
The fresh ocean breezes, our young faces tanned.
We'd join in the play there in sheer delight
And oft lingered on, till day turned to night.

On hillsides we roamed, by the brooks and the streams
And weaned there with rapture, our young boyhood dreams,
While brooklet and stream would meander along
To meet with the river, so rugged and strong.

I see in my dreams now the soft morning dew
Descended on mountains, I loved and I knew.
Then gently the rising sun kissed it away
To break forth once more into beautiful day.

Farewell then, dear Wales, the land that prompts dreams
And bring deep contentment, though childish it seems,
Those valleys and mountains forever will be
A source of great pleasure and comfort to me.

William. T. Owen

Night Shades

Slowly the Sun sinks low in the west,
Birds softly coo to each other at rest.
Twilight is creeping o'er Moorland and Fell,
Darkness is stealing on Hilltop and Dell.

Birds soar up high to their nests in the trees,
Filling the air with such sweet melodies.
Children are climbing the stairs to their beds,
In peaceful slumber to lay down their heads.

Toilers to home weary footsteps now wends,
Seeking the comfort of loved ones and friends.
Joy and contentment is waiting them there,
Pleasure and kindness not found ev'rywhere.

Soon weary bodies relax in their chairs,
Watching the coal in the fire as it flares.
Peaceful their thoughts as the warmth steals their way
And soon ends for them, a long weary day.

William. T. Owen
Oct. 1939

Sleep Well

Sleep well, my dearest child
In slumber close thine eyes,
While Mother softly sings to thee
Sweet charming lullabies.

May guarding angels, sweet
Their constant vigil keep
Throughout the night, may peace be thine
In calm, reposing sleep.

Sleep well, my dearest child
The night will soon be gone
And thou shall wake with morning light
To hear the sweet bird's song.

William. T. Owen

Larks' Lament

The larks have flown from Westwood Meadow,
The grassland gone and every hedgerow.
The lofty climbers lost their home
To bricks and mortar, hearts of stone.
Social climbers with airy lofts
Are roosting now in beds so soft,
Tucking in their two point four,
Where once rose voices sweet and pure.

Fly forever fast and free,
This is how I want to be,
Ever higher sure and proud!
Ariel's guardians of the clouds.

The larks are gone from Westwood Heath,
Empty skies with bricks beneath.
The builder's laugh and Georgians mock
To see who has now taken stock
Of Farthing Walk and Shilling Drive,
Two legged folks there now abide,
Where once flew beauty wild and free,
Left only now in memory.

Fly forever fast and free,
This is how I want to be,
Ever higher sure and proud!
Ariel's guardians of the clouds.

19th April 2006

Urban Fox

I appreciate your kindness and the scraps you leave outside,
Thank you for the shelter under your shed my cubs reside.
Some, they call us vermin and they kill without a care
But there surely is a place for all on this planet we do share.
I once had fields in which to roam and mice and worms to eat
But now your trains and houses are where I trod my feet.
So, I ask you who are vermin now, as you sprawl across the Earth?
Please spare a thought for others and don't leave us with this dearth.

For Sam
27th November 2023

Mother Earth

Would you burn the bed you sleep in?
Would you choke the air you breathe?
Would you poison children's water?
Would you bite the hand that feeds?
Would you turn against your brother?
Would you trash your neighbourhood?
Would you let them rape your mother?
Would you sell a sister's love?

Wake up, wake up, wake up, open your eyes,
Wake up, wake up, before our Mother dies.
The world, her voice is screaming,
Our Mother she is pleading,
Wake up, wake up, please listen to her cries.

Can you stop the world and get off?
Can you fly off to the stars?
Can you float around the ether?
Can you make a home on Mars?
Can you turn back time- press reset?
Can you live eternally?
Can you dwell inside a bubble?
Can you simply run and flee?

Wake up, wake up, wake up, open your eyes,
Wake up, wake up, before our Mother dies.
The world, her voice is screaming,
Our Mother she is pleading,
Wake up, wake up, don't listen to their lies.

I've said it once, I've said it twice
And now I'll say it thrice,
Please hear my voice, remember well
And heed my free advice.
This world we live on is not ours
To pillage rape and burn,
We are the caretakers for all,
When will we ever learn?

18th July 2019

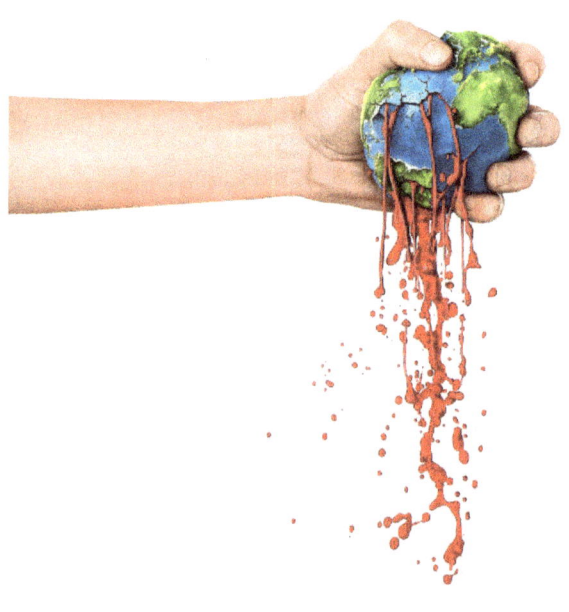

Riversong

As we meander throughout life,
Sometimes with ease, sometimes with strife,
Our journey mirrors the river's course,
Pushed along by nature's force.
Like driftwood bobbing upon the tide,
Jostled and bumped by the river's ride,
Sometimes we have to just let go
And see which way the waters flow.
We are born from crystal springs,
Our energy one with everything.
With all creation we entwine,
We are the sum of love divine.

Our ripples spreading throughout time,
Touching souls and touching minds,
Forever outwards far and wide,
Decisions affecting people's lives.
The eddies left upon your wake,
Encircle me now- each choice I make,
I'll skim a stone in your memory
And always know what will be, will be.
We are born from crystal springs,
Our energy one with everything.
With all creation we entwine,
We are the sum of love divine.

I heard your voice in the river's tune
And watched your spirit ride the spume.
As the water turned to burnished bronze,
The river sang its sweet, sweet song.
The rock pools shone with mercury
And I saw you leaping, oh, so free.
The dolphins lead you o'er the bar
And guided you towards your star.
We are born from crystal springs,
Our energy one with everything.
With all creation we entwine,
We are the sum of love divine.

05th November 2006

Dogs Are Awesome

Dogs are awesome, dogs are great,
They really are your very best mate.
They'll stick with you through thick and thin
And look on you as their own kin.

Dogs are awesome, dogs are kind,
They help you when you're in a bind.
They'll be your eyes when you can't see
And just be there for company.

Dogs are awesome, dogs are grand,
They comfort you- paw in hand.
They'll use their nose to tell the time
And sometimes seem to read your mind.

Dogs are awesome, dogs are brill,
They have many a unique skill.
They'll even help to detect cancer
And always give an honest answer.

Dogs are awesome, dogs are cool,
They lick your face and share their drool.
They'll let you know if you're in danger
And protect you from a harmful stranger.

Dogs are awesome, dogs are fun,
Their devotion you've surely won.
And loyalty they've truly mastered,
Unlike cats- the selfish bastards!
                    13th November 2023

The Hind and the Hunter

She stands so proud, the gentle doe,
Her coat reflects the moon's soft glow,
Her breath, so still, stands on the air,
The Winter snow on coat so fair.
A pallid ghost amongst the trees,
A living wraith, forever free.
Regal, serene, Queen of the land,
Embodiment of nature's hand.

He sits so proud, the mighty man,
Hunter, taker of all he can.
Arrogant, strong, Regent of all Thule,
Embodiment of tyrant's rule.
Haughty, aloof, the mighty King
Claims ownership of everything.
His voice is heard throughout the land
And all do quake under his hand.

The doe she stares with limpid gaze
Upon the man with hateful ways
And wonders at the cruelty
Cast upon those with spirits free.
Anger flashes across his eyes,
Like lightening flared through midnight skies
And shadows pass across his face,
Whilst murderous clouds from Hades race.

She bounds away into the wood,
Far from her fate if she but could.
With gleeful cry he fast pursues
Towards his trophy of palest hue.
Onwards she runs into the dark,
The hunter's sight upon his mark,
Deeper and deeper into the brush,
Doe and hunter both do rush.

Forwards on, never looking back,
Senses alert for the attack,
The brave young doe she gallops long,
Drawing this man who'll do her wrong,
Far away from those held dear,
This night of terror hers to bear,
For she alone will pay the cost
Of crossing paths with one so lost.

At last, she can no longer run
And turns to face mans' wretched son.
Standing square she stares him down,
Mythical Goddess with fairest gown.
Raising his bow with insane glee,
Notching an arrow, he sets it free.
The missile flies both straight and true,
Piercing her heart, it kills the doe.

The hind she falls upon the ground,
With otherworldly screaming sound.
A noise so terrible to hear,
That those who harken flee in fear.
The King's good steed with dreadful fright,
Bolts far away into the night.
Leaving the stricken, gentle, doe.
Blood spattered - garnets in the snow.

On and on the horse does race,
As Regent clings with steely face,
Until the path by branch is blocked
And from his seat the King is knocked.
His stirrup holding fast his boot,
He vainly tries to free his foot.
When boulder hard upon the ground
Strikes down the king and breaks his crown.

The bloody corpse with foot still stuck,
Bounces along through mud and muck.
The trappings of one royal born
Now soiled and damaged, ripped and torn.
The horse he gallops homeward bound
And there the battered king is found
In such a sad and sorry state,
Grand ruler now has met his fate.

The gentle Prince with eyes so blue,
Is woken up and told the news.
For he was born now to succeed
This monstrous man of word and deed.
But the Prince's heart was filled with good
And so, he vowed, if he but could,
To rule not like his sire before
But with compassion and honest lore.

For the King had broken ancient code
This night by murdering the doe
And his now is the vital quest
To wrong the right and do his best
To herald peace and harmony,
For all the souls in his country.
And solemnly he makes the choice
To speak for those without a voice.

The heavy clouds now spent and gone
And evil deeds now truly done,
On horizon breaks the faintest light,
To truly quash this foulest night.
The sunlight stirs a young, pale fawn,
A brand new day for her does dawn
Because her dam did sacrifice,
For her to live; her very life.

11th January 2024

Reciprocity

I share with you, you share with me,
That is reciprocity.
For good of all -it's plain to see,
Back and forth mutually.
Equal rights, resources free,
A concept of simplicity.
Compassion really is the key,
That is reciprocity.

2nd December 2023

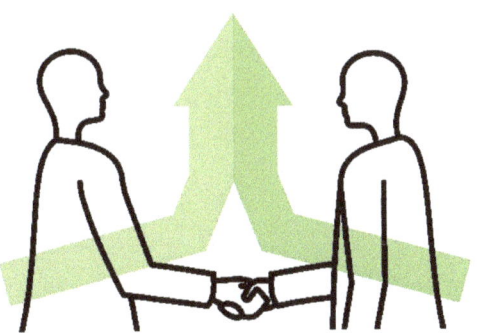

One Medicine

In ancient times gone by a remedy was a remedy.
No distinction between folk, now a distant memory.
The rise of Western medicine brought a great divide,
Nineteenth Century medics cast animals aside.
Vets went one way and doctor surgeons the other,
No collaboration or shared knowledge, neither side did bother.

But an eye is an eye and a tooth is a tooth,
Beit animal or human, most do have both.
Skin, bone, muscle, brain, kidneys, liver and heart.
Fear, pain, love, joy; there's little to tell us apart.

And here we are in current times, the parties still work alone.
Animals tested for curative finds, we really now must atone.
For what it the point of seeking a cure if one already exists?
Now is the time to sit down and talk and needless killing desist.
When resources are pooled, advancements they will jettison,
So, shout out now, a voice for all and the concept of One Medicine.

For an eye is an eye and a tooth is a tooth,
Beit animal or human, most do have both.
Skin, bone, muscle, brain, kidneys, liver and heart.
Fear, pain, love, joy; there's little to tell us apart.

07th January 2024

I believe that animals and humans have an equal right to exist on this earth and there should be no discrimination when it comes to food, shelter, protection or medicine. As the dominant species and guardians of this planet, it is our duty of care to ensure that all her inhabitants get a fair deal.

I am an Ambassador for Humanimal Trust (a charity that seeks to bring human and animal medicine together for the reciprocal benefit of all parties) and will be donating the royalties from this book to them. Please check out their website for more information about them and the brilliant work that they do.

https://www.humanimaltrust.org.uk/

Milton Keynes UK
Ingram Content Group UK Ltd.
UKHW052251270924
448904UK00010B/91